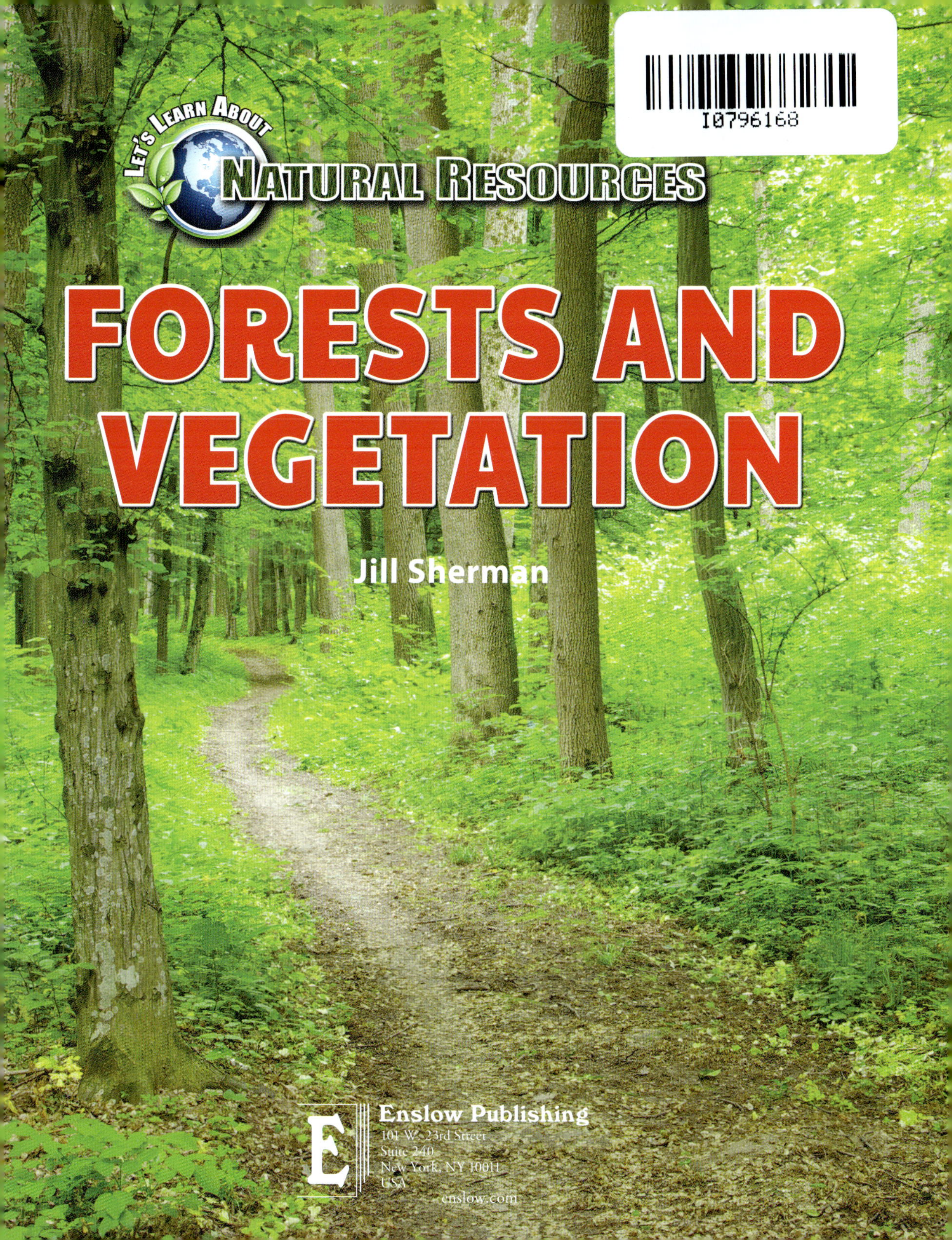
I0796168
Let's Learn About
Natural Resources
FORESTS AND VEGETATION
Jill Sherman
Enslow Publishing
101 W. 23rd Street
Suite 240
New York, NY 10011
USA
enslow.com

Words to Know

logging The business of cutting down trees to sell the wood for building homes and structures.

natural resource Something from nature that people use.

oxygen cycle The cycle in which oxygen is used and replenished in our environment.

recycle To use something again.

renewable Something that can be replenished.

Contents

Our Green World

Plants are a big part of our world. You can find them almost anywhere. Plants make up our forests. They grow in harsh deserts. They are even in the icy tundra.

FAST FACT
Scientists know of about 400,000 different kinds of plants on Earth.

A Growing Resource

We get everything we need from the earth. Plants are a great natural resource. From farms to forests, we rely on plants for many things.

FAST FACT
Plant resources are renewable. New plants can grow. They take the place of others that were cut down or died.

Plants Feed Us

What's on your dinner plate?

A bowl of pasta with tomato sauce?

A spicy dish of rice and beans?

A fresh salad with crunchy cucumbers?

So much of our food comes from plants.

Fast Fact

About 11 percent of the world's land is used to grow crops.

The Oxygen Cycle

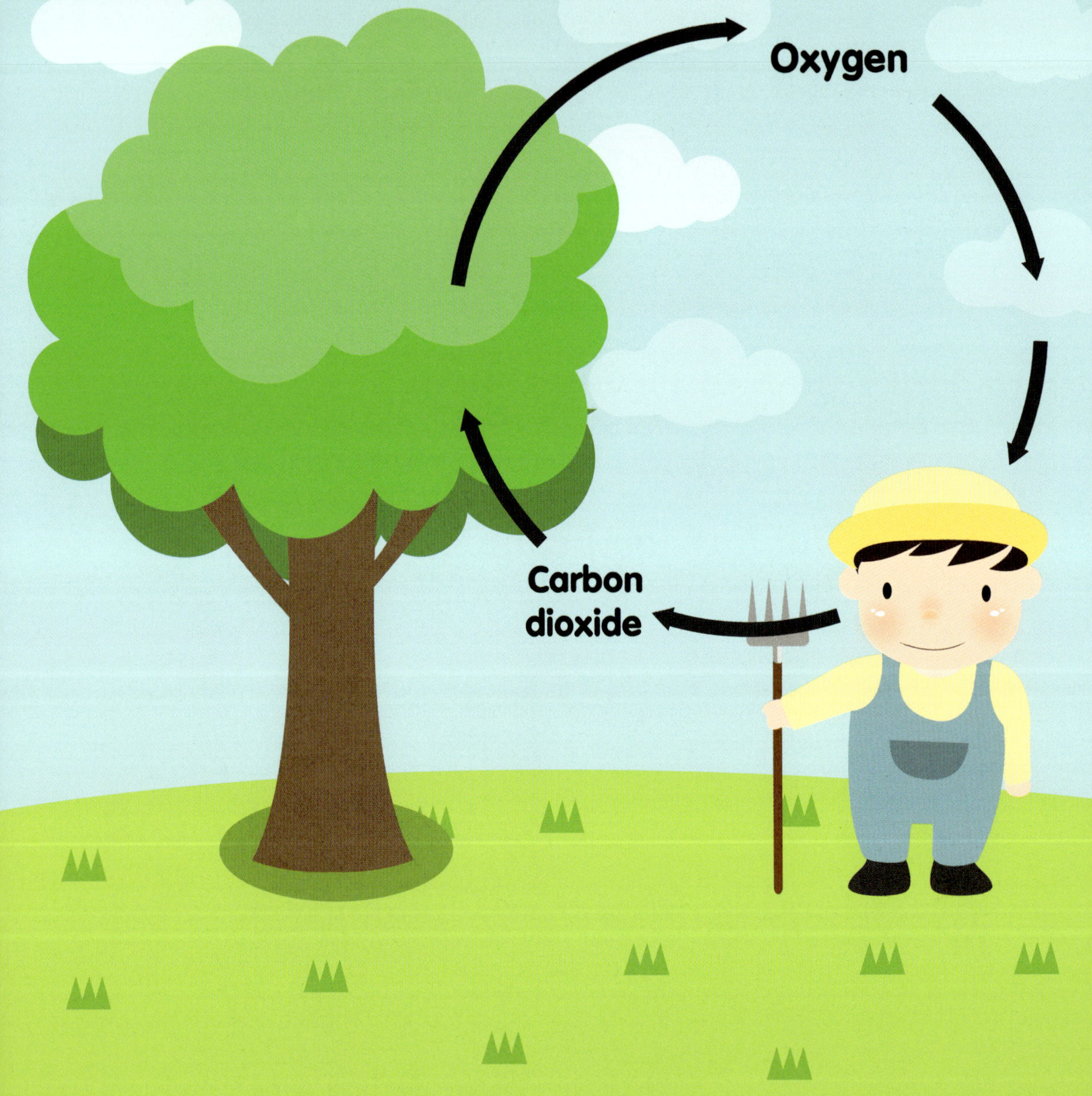

Oxygen Makers

Without plants you wouldn't be able to breathe. They play a key role in the oxygen cycle. We use earth's air. People and animals breathe in oxygen. Then, they breathe out carbon dioxide. Plants take in carbon dioxide. They release oxygen.

Fast Fact
All animals need oxygen. Even fish use oxygen, which they take in from the water.

From the Forest

Right now, you are holding a plant product. The paper in this book came from a tree. Wood is used in many products. From your school desk to the pencil in your hand, wood helps build our world.

Plants in Products

Some plant products might surprise you. Think about your bike's tires and the soles of your shoes. Rubber comes from plants. What about your favorite T-shirt? It came from the cotton plant! Plants are hiding in many everyday products.

Nature's Medicine Cabinet

Plants are great medicine. Ingredients from plants treat pain, heal wounds, and fight cancer. Scientists study plants. The next great cure could soon be unlocked!

FAST FACT
People have been using plants as medicine for at least 5,000 years.

Forests in Danger

Thousands of trees are cut down every day. But it takes many years for a new tree to grow. Because of logging, our forests are disappearing.

FAST FACT
You use about seven trees each year in paper, wood, and other products.

Save the Forests

Most paper is made from wood. By recycling paper, fewer trees will need to be cut down. Replanting trees also helps keep forests alive.

FAST FACT
If all our newspapers were recycled, we could save 250 million trees every year!

Activity

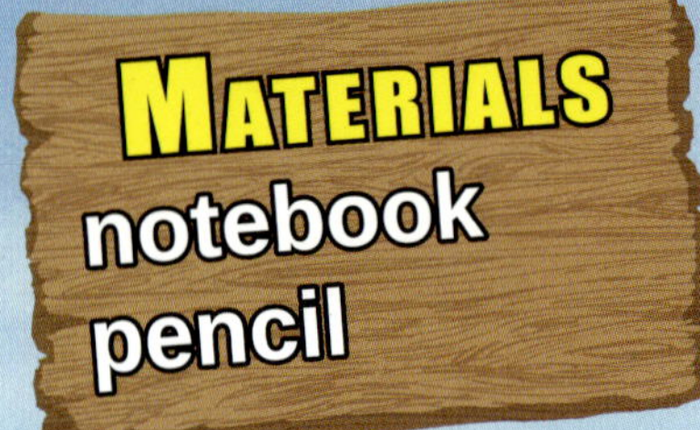

NATURE WALK

Procedure:

1. With an adult, research your state tree. Find out what its leaves and bark look like.

2. Make notes about these details in your notebook.

3. Visit a park and go for a nature hike.

4. Consult your notes and see if you can spot your state's tree.

Learn More

Books

Agarwal, Tanya Luther. *Weird and Wonderful: Fruits and Vegetables.* New Delhi, India: The Energy and Resources Institute, 2015.

Bagai, Shona. *Science in Our Environment: Plant Kingdom.* New Delhi, India: The Energy and Resources Institute, 2015.

Lundgren, Julie K. *Plants as Food, Fuel, and Medicine.* Vero Beach, FL: Rourke Educational Media, 2014.

Websites

Earth Matters!
earthmatters4kids.org/main.html
Learn more about healthy food and water.

Easy Science For Kids
easyscienceforkids.com/all-about-forests/
Read some fun facts about forests.

National Geographic Kids
kids.nationalgeographic.com/explore/celebrations/earth-day/#earth-day-cleanup.jpg
Discover the simple things you can do to help the planet.

Index

Published in 2018 by Enslow Publishing, LLC.
101 W. 23rd Street, Suite 240, New York, NY 10011

Library of Congress Cataloging-in-Publication Data
Names: Sherman, Jill.
Title: Forests and vegetation / Jill Sherman.
Description: New York : Enslow Publishing, 2018. | Series: Let's learn about natural resources | Audience: Grades K–3. | Includes bibliographical references and index.
Identifiers: LCCN 2017011311| ISBN 9780766093836 (pbk.) | ISBN 9780766093843 (6 pack) | ISBN 9780766092372 (library bound)
Subjects: LCSH: Forest ecology—Juvenile literature. | Forest conservation—Juvenile literature.
Classification: LCC QH541.5.F6 S4329 2018 | DDC 577.3—dc23

LC record available at https://lccn.loc.gov/2017011311

Printed in China

Photo Credits: Cover, pp. 1, 4 irin-k/Shutterstock.com; interior pages (soil, grass, sky) Andrey_Kuzmin/Shutterstock.com; interior pages (sign) johavel/Shutterstock.com; p. 6 absolutimages/Shutterstock.com; p. 8 michaeljung/Shutterstock.com; p. 10 Preeda340/Shutterstock.com; p. 12 Tracy Whiteside/Shutterstock.com; p. 14 Ronnachai Palas/Shutterstock.com; p. 16 Stokkete/Shutterstock.com; p. 18 TFoxFoto/Shutterstock.com; p. 20 Air Images/Shutterstock.com; p. 23 Monkey Business Images/Shutterstock.com.